VICTORIAN SPIRITUALISM

Victorian Spiritualism

BRYAN PETERS

Victorian Spiritualism

Introduction: A Personal Journey into Spiritualism

My life as a medium has been deeply intertwined with the spiritual, mysterious, and unseen. Victorian Spiritualism isn't just a historical curiosity—it's the foundation of the path that I walk today. It has shaped how I experience the world, how I communicate with those who have passed, and how I understand life, death, and the ethereal space that connects us all. As a practicing medium, I see myself as part of an ongoing tradition that began long before my time and continues to evolve as we deepen our understanding of the afterlife.

Spiritualism is not simply a belief in ghosts or spirits, nor is it just a fascination with death. It is a practice, a philosophy, and a way of being that bridges the material and the immaterial, the seen and the unseen. The Victorian Spiritualist movement, which began in the mid-19th century, sparked a renewed interest in life beyond death and gave form to a tradition that endures to this day. Through this booklet, I invite you to join me on a journey through the history of this movement, its philosophies, its rituals, and its legacy, both in my life and in the broader fabric of American society.

The Personal Connection: My Role as a Medium

For those unfamiliar with the term, a medium is someone who acts as an intermediary between the living and the spirits of those who have passed away. This communication may take many forms, including verbal messages, physical sensations, or emotional impressions. Mediumship is not a new practice; it exists in various forms across cultures and throughout history. However, in Victorian America, Spiritualism brought mediumship into the public eye in a way it had never been before. It became not only a personal or religious practice but a social phenomenon.

I became aware of my ability to communicate with the spirit world at a young age. It began with small, inexplicable experiences—objects moving, voices calling my name, or feelings that couldn't be attributed to anything in the physical world. As I grew older, these experiences intensified, and I came to understand that the voices and presences I felt were not figments of my imagination but real communications from those who had crossed over to the other side. I didn't choose this path—it chose me. And once I accepted this calling, I knew I had found my place within the long tradition of mediums who had walked this path before me.

Victorian Spiritualism, for me, was not simply a historical movement; it was a way to understand my gift and my role in the world. The mediums of the 19th century paved the way for people like me, normalizing spirit communication and offering a framework through which we could connect with the dead. These pioneers took something that had always existed in the shadows and brought it into the light of day, where it could be discussed, examined, and embraced by a wider community.

The Spark of Spiritualism in America

The story of Victorian Spiritualism in America is one of hope, curiosity, and a deep yearning for connection. It began in an unassuming home in Hydesville, New York, where two young sisters—Margaret and Kate Fox—claimed to hear mysterious knocking sounds that they believed were communications from the spirit world. This event, known as the "Hydesville Rappings," is often cited as the birth of the Spiritualist movement. But this was just the beginning.

The Fox Sisters' discovery ignited a firestorm of interest across the United States. In the midst of a rapidly industrializing and modernizing society, people were beginning to question traditional religious structures and were looking for new ways to understand the mysteries of life and death. Spiritualism provided a way to connect with loved ones who had passed and to explore the unknown realms of the afterlife. It promised not just the hope of continued existence after death but actual communication with those who had crossed over.

As I reflect on the early days of Spiritualism, I am reminded of how similar the experiences of the Fox Sisters were to my own early experiences. The knocking, the inexplicable sensations, the feeling that someone unseen was trying to communicate—it was as if the universe was reminding me that I am part of something much larger. The Hydesville Rappings may have been the catalyst for the Victorian Spiritualist movement, but they were also a reminder that the spirit world is never far from us.

Spiritualism in a Changing America

The 19th century was a time of immense change in America. The nation was grappling with the expansion of its territories, the horrors of slavery, and the devastation of the Civil War. Amidst this turmoil, Spiritualism offered a sense of comfort and continuity. For families who had lost loved ones in battle, for women who had lost children to disease, and for individuals who felt disconnected from traditional religious institutions, Spiritualism provided a way to stay connected to those who had passed.

This was a time when grief was deeply woven into the fabric of daily life. Victorian mourning rituals were elaborate, often lasting for months or even years. The presence of death was constant, yet traditional religious teachings offered little more than the promise of a far-off heaven or hell. Spiritualism, by contrast, suggested that the dead were not gone at all—that they remained nearby, still able to communicate, still able to provide comfort and guidance to the living. This was a radical departure from conventional religious thought, and it struck a chord with many who were searching for answers in a world that seemed increasingly uncertain.

The movement attracted a wide array of followers, from working-class individuals to intellectuals and even prominent public figures. It provided a space where women, in particular, could take on leadership roles, both as mediums and as advocates for social change. Many Spiritualists were also involved in other progressive movements of the time, including abolitionism, women's suffrage, and the temperance movement. The messages they received from the spirit world were often intertwined with calls for justice and equality in the physical world.

The Purpose of This Booklet

This booklet is an exploration of the history, philosophy, and rituals of Victorian Spiritualism, as well as its ongoing legacy in contemporary America. As a practicing medium, I offer not just a historical overview but a personal perspective on what it means to walk between the worlds of the living and the dead. We will look at the pioneers of the movement, the tools and practices they used, and the ways in which Spiritualism shaped, and was shaped by, the broader currents of American society.

Through the pages that follow, we will journey through the history of the movement, from its origins in a small farmhouse in Hydesville to its spread across the nation and the world. We will examine the key figures who shaped the movement, the controversies that surrounded it, and the ways in which it has continued to evolve over time. And, along the way, I will share my own experiences as a medium, offering insights into how the practices of Victorian Spiritualism continue to inform and inspire my work today.

Spiritualism is not just a relic of the past; it is a living, breathing practice that continues to offer comfort, wisdom, and connection to those who seek it. I hope that by the end of this journey, you too will feel the presence of the spirits that surround us, offering their guidance and support from beyond the veil.

The Birth of Spiritualism: The Fox Sisters and the Hydesville Rappings

The story of Victorian Spiritualism begins in 1848 in the small town of Hydesville, New York, where two young sisters, Margaret and Kate Fox, claimed to experience communication from the spirit world. The Fox family had moved into a house with a dark history—a history that would soon come to light through a series of strange and unexplainable occurrences.

One night in March 1848, the Fox sisters began hearing mysterious knocking sounds or "rappings" within their home. At first, the family assumed these were natural sounds—a creaking floorboard, the settling of the house—but the rappings persisted, growing louder and more insistent. Eventually, the sisters realized that the noises responded to them, as if something, or someone, was attempting to communicate. This was no ordinary disturbance; it was the beginning of what would become known as the Hydesville Rappings, and it marked the birth of modern Spiritualism.

The sisters devised a simple system for communicating with the spirit, asking it to knock once for "yes" and twice for "no." The entity claimed to be the spirit of a peddler who had been murdered and buried in the basement of their house. The Fox Sisters' ability to interact with the spirit world soon attracted local attention. Neighbors gathered to witness the rappings, and word of the phenomena quickly spread beyond the small village of Hydesville. People were intrigued, amazed, and sometimes frightened by the idea that the dead could speak through these young girls.

While skeptics questioned the authenticity of the Fox sisters' experiences, believers flocked to their home, desperate to hear from their own deceased loved ones. The sisters' communication with spirits was viewed as a doorway into the unknown, and what was once considered impossible suddenly seemed attainable. The event electrified American society, sparking a wave of interest in the possibility of life after death.

What set the Fox sisters apart from other mediums who had practiced in secret or in small, isolated communities was their ability to bring spirit communication into the public eye. Before this event, mediumship and the belief in communication with the dead were often relegated to the fringes of society, seen as superstitious or taboo. The Hydesville Rappings, however, occurred at a time of great social change in America, when the nation was open to new ideas and eager for answers that neither religion nor science could provide.

As the popularity of the Fox sisters grew, they began to hold public séances, attracting even more attention. It wasn't long before other mediums emerged, each with their own unique abilities to communicate with the dead. Spiritualism quickly evolved into a national movement, with adherents seeking out mediums to connect with lost family members, gain insight into the afterlife, or even seek guidance from famous figures who had passed on.

For me, the Fox Sisters' story resonates deeply. It's not just about two young girls discovering that the spirit world exists—it's about the moment when the veil between the living and the dead was torn wide open, allowing the rest of us to glimpse what lies beyond. This is why the Fox sisters are so important to the history of Spiritualism. They showed the world that the spirits are always close and always willing to speak, if we are willing to listen.

Though the sisters faced scrutiny and accusations of fraud later in life, their impact on the Spiritualist movement cannot be overstated. They gave the movement its spark, igniting a flame that continues to burn today. For mediums like myself, their story is a reminder that we are part of a long tradition—a tradition of seeking truth in the unknown, of listening for the whispers of the past, and of carrying forward the messages of those who have left this world.

The Philosophy Behind Spiritualism: Death Is Not the End

While the public was fascinated by the dramatic phenomena of séances and spirit communication, Spiritualism's
enduring power lay in its philosophy. For Spiritualists, death
was not an end but a transition, a crossing from one realm
of existence into another. The soul, in their view, does not
perish but continues to grow, learn, and evolve in the afterlife. This belief was not only comforting to those who had
lost loved ones but also offered a radically different view of
existence itself.

The roots of this philosophy can be traced to a variety of
intellectual and religious influences, from Christian mysticism to Mesmerism, and particularly the works of Andrew
Jackson Davis. Davis, often referred to as the "John the Baptist of Spiritualism," was a clairvoyant and mystic whose
writings provided much of the theoretical framework for the
movement. His book *The Principles of Nature, Her Divine Revelations, and A Voice to Mankind* laid out a vision of the universe in which the material and spiritual worlds were deeply
interconnected.

Davis claimed to receive his insights directly from the
spirit world, and his work blended elements of Transcendentalism, Christian mysticism, and science. He posited that
the spirit world was a natural extension of the material one,
not a distant, inaccessible place. According to Davis, the
soul continues to evolve after death, moving through various planes of existence, each one offering new opportunities for growth and enlightenment. This was a radical
departure from the traditional Christian views of heaven and

hell, and it resonated with many who felt disillusioned by orthodox religion.

The idea that death is not the end is central to Spiritualist philosophy, and it has profound implications for how we live our lives. If we believe that our souls will continue to exist after our physical bodies die, then we must consider what kind of existence we are creating for ourselves in the afterlife. Spiritualism teaches that our thoughts, actions, and choices in this life influence our spiritual development in the next. This belief fosters a sense of responsibility, not just for our physical lives but for our spiritual well-being.

For me as a medium, this philosophy is not an abstract concept—it is a lived experience. Every time I communicate with a spirit, I am reminded that the soul's journey does not end with death. The spirits I encounter are not static; they are still learning, growing, and evolving, just as we are. Some spirits come forward seeking to offer guidance and wisdom, while others are still processing the lessons of their earthly lives. In this way, the afterlife is not so different from our current existence. It is simply another stage in the soul's eternal journey.

Victorian Spiritualists also believed that by communicating with spirits, they could gain insights into the nature of the afterlife and the deeper truths of existence. Mediums were seen not just as channels for communication but as spiritual guides who could help others understand the mysteries of life and death. The messages that came through during séances were often deeply philosophical, offering perspectives on morality, love, justice, and the purpose of life. In this way, Spiritualism became more than just a way to connect with the dead—it became a path to spiritual growth and enlightenment.

This belief in the continuity of the soul also offered comfort to those who were grieving. In the 19th century, death was a constant presence in daily life. Infant mortality rates were high, and diseases such as tuberculosis claimed many lives at a young age. The Civil War, in particular, left countless families mourning the loss of loved ones. Traditional Christian teachings offered little more than the promise of eventual reunion in heaven, but Spiritualism offered something more immediate. The dead were not far away; they were still present, still able to communicate, still watching over the living.

For many grieving families, this belief provided solace in a time of great loss. Séances became a way to not only connect with deceased loved ones but also to gain reassurance that they were at peace and that the bond between the living and the dead had not been broken. As a medium, I have witnessed firsthand the power of this belief. When I connect someone with a loved one who has passed, I see the relief and comfort that comes from knowing that death is not the end, that their loved one is still with them in spirit.

The philosophy of Spiritualism continues to resonate today. In a world where traditional religious beliefs often feel disconnected from modern life, Spiritualism offers a way to explore the mysteries of existence without rejecting science or reason. It is a belief system that encourages personal exploration, spiritual growth, and a deep connection to the world around us, both seen and unseen. For those who seek answers to life's most profound questions, Spiritualism offers a path of discovery that goes beyond the boundaries of conventional thought.

Séances: The Rituals of Spirit Communication

At the heart of Spiritualist practice is the séance, a ritual in which the living attempt to communicate with the spirits of the dead. For those unfamiliar with this practice, a séance might seem like something out of a horror movie—dark rooms, strange voices, objects moving of their own accord. But for mediums like myself, séances are sacred spaces where the veil between the living and the dead is thinned, and meaningful connections can be made.

Victorian séances were elaborate affairs, often held in dimly lit parlors or specially designed séance rooms. Participants would gather in a circle, holding hands to create a chain of energy that would help facilitate spirit communication. The medium would act as a conduit, channeling the energy of the spirits and allowing them to communicate through various means, such as rappings, voices, or even physical manifestations.

The tools used in these séances were as varied as the mediums themselves. One of the most commonly used instruments was the spirit trumpet, a cone-shaped device that helped amplify the voice of the spirit. Mediums also used planchettes and automatic writing to allow spirits to convey messages. In some cases, spirits would manifest physically, appearing as luminous figures or moving objects within the room. These phenomena were known as "physical mediumship" and were a major focus of Victorian Spiritualism.

As a modern medium, I continue to use many of these traditional tools in my work, though I also rely heavily on my own intuitive abilities. When I enter a séance, I open myself to the energies of the spirits present, allowing them to communicate through me. This process can take many forms—sometimes I receive clear messages in the form of words or images, while other times I experience physical sensations that the spirit wishes to convey. No two séances are ever the same, and each one is a unique experience for both the medium and the participants.

Famous Mediums and Their Impact on the Movement

The Victorian Spiritualist movement produced many famous mediums whose work shaped the course of the movement and brought it to the attention of the wider public. Among the most well-known were figures like Emma Hardinge Britten, Cora L. V. Scott, and Daniel Dunglas Home, each of whom contributed to the development of Spiritualism in their own way.

Emma Hardinge Britten was a British medium and spiritualist who became one of the leading voices of the movement in the 19th century. She was known for her trance lectures, during which she would enter a deep state of trance and deliver sermons and teachings from the spirit world. Her work helped establish Spiritualism as not just a practice but a coherent philosophical system that offered a new way of understanding life, death, and the afterlife.

Cora L. V. Scott, often referred to as "The Little Medium," was a child prodigy who began giving public mediumistic demonstrations at the age of 14. She became one of the most popular and respected mediums in America, drawing large crowds to her séances and lectures. Scott's ability to communicate with spirits and deliver eloquent sermons while in a trance state made her a key figure in the spread of Spiritualism.

Daniel Dunglas Home, a Scottish medium, was perhaps the most famous of the Victorian era. His séances were renowned for their extraordinary physical phenomena, including levitations, the appearance of ghostly hands, and even the movement of furniture without any apparent cause. Home was investigated by numerous skeptics but was never definitively proven to be a fraud, which only added to his mystique. His work helped legitimize Spiritualism in the eyes of the public, and he became a key figure in the movement's growth.

The Tools of Mediumship: The Spirit Trumpet and Spirit Cabinet

Victorian Spiritualism was not only marked by the individuals who led the movement but also by the unique tools and instruments they used to facilitate communication with the spirit world. Two of the most fascinating and iconic tools were the spirit trumpet and the spirit cabinet. Both served as physical conduits to amplify spiritual energies and allow for more potent connections between mediums and spirits.

The spirit trumpet, shaped like a megaphone, was often placed in the center of the séance circle. Participants believed that the trumpet could amplify the voices of spirits, making it easier for the living to hear their messages. In some séances, the trumpet would move on its own, levitating above the table, spinning, or pointing toward specific participants as the spirits directed it. This mysterious movement was seen as confirmation that a spirit was present and actively engaging with the group.

As a practicing medium, I've found that the spirit trumpet is a powerful symbol of focus and intent. While I don't always use the trumpet in modern séances, its presence still evokes the historical depth of Spiritualism and serves as a reminder of the power that can be accessed during these gatherings. The trumpet is a physical manifestation of the idea that communication between the realms is possible, and that sound, the most basic of vibrations, can cross between dimensions.

Another critical tool was the spirit cabinet. This was a small, often curtained enclosure where the medium would sit during the séance. The purpose of the spirit cabinet was to concentrate the medium's energies and reduce external distractions, creating a space in which the spirits could manifest more easily. In many Victorian séances, objects within the cabinet would move, disembodied voices would speak, or lights would appear as the spirits made their presence known.

In my practice, the concept of the spirit cabinet translates to creating a sacred space—a place where both the medium and the participants can focus on the energy of the séance. Whether it's a designated room, a table with meaningful objects, or even just a quiet corner of a home, having a focused space for spiritual work is essential. It allows the medium to center their energy, while giving the spirits a place to gather and communicate.

These tools—the spirit trumpet and the spirit cabinet—were not just gimmicks or novelties; they were essential components of the Spiritualist practice. They represented the belief that the spirit world was just a breath away and that, with the right focus and tools, communication between the living and the dead could be facilitated. Even today, these objects are revered by Spiritualists for the sense of mystery and awe they bring to the practice.

Women and Spiritualism: A Path to Empowerment

One of the most remarkable aspects of Victorian Spiritualism was the prominent role women played in its development. During a time when women were largely excluded from positions of power, both socially and politically, Spiritualism provided a platform for female empowerment. Many of the most influential mediums of the 19th century were women, and their leadership within the movement allowed them to defy societal norms and take on roles of authority and influence.

In the rigid structure of Victorian society, women were often relegated to the private sphere, confined to roles as wives, mothers, and caretakers. Public speaking, leadership, and intellectual engagement were domains dominated by men. However, Spiritualism provided women with a unique opportunity. As mediums, women were not only seen as spiritually gifted but also as leaders in a growing religious movement. They were able to stand before audiences, deliver powerful messages, and guide others in their spiritual journeys.

For many women, Spiritualism offered an avenue to explore their spirituality and intellect outside the constraints of the church and traditional society. Figures like Emma Hardinge Britten, Cora L. V. Scott, and the Fox Sisters were trailblazers, using their mediumistic abilities to command respect and attention in a world that otherwise sought to silence them.

Cora L. V. Scott, for example, became known as one of the most gifted trance speakers of her time. From a young age, she traveled across the United States, delivering sermons and lectures on spiritual matters while in a trance state. Her ability to communicate complex spiritual ideas while in trance gained her a following and a level of authority that was rare for women of her era.

For me, as a modern medium, this legacy is a profound source of inspiration. The women who led the Spiritualist movement paved the way for future generations of women to explore their spiritual gifts and claim their space in religious and social spheres. Spiritualism, with its focus on equality in spiritual matters, allowed women to lead and be heard. It provided a counter-narrative to the male-dominated religious institutions of the time, where women's voices were often marginalized.

Moreover, the alignment of Spiritualism with other social reform movements of the 19th century, such as abolitionism and women's suffrage, further strengthened its appeal to progressive-minded women. Many Spiritualist women, including Susan B. Anthony and Elizabeth Cady Stanton, were deeply involved in both the Spiritualist movement and the fight for women's rights. They saw Spiritualism as a path not only for personal spiritual empowerment but also for societal change.

The connection between Spiritualism and women's rights was no accident. The belief in communication with spirits, particularly with those who had passed on, often brought messages of equality, justice, and reform. For many mediums and their followers, these messages from the spirit world were seen as divine endorsements of the need for social change.

In my own practice, I carry forward the legacy of these women who came before me. They remind me that being a medium is not just about personal connection with the spirit world—it's about being part of a larger movement for empowerment, truth, and social justice. The spirits often bring messages of healing, forgiveness, and growth, but they also remind us of the importance of standing up for what is right and just in this world.

Spiritualism continues to be a space where women can lead, heal, and connect with the divine on their own terms. It's a tradition that honors the feminine in a way that few other religious movements have historically done, and for that, it remains a vital source of empowerment for women today.

The Role of Skepticism: Faith and Fraud in Spiritualism

No discussion of Victorian Spiritualism would be complete without addressing the skepticism and controversy that surrounded the movement from its inception. From the very beginning, there were those who doubted the legitimacy of spirit communication and accused mediums of trickery, fraud, or outright deceit. The tension between faith and skepticism was a central theme of the Spiritualist movement, and it remains a key issue in modern mediumship as well.

The rise of Spiritualism coincided with a period of intense scientific inquiry in the Western world. The 19th century saw great advances in technology, medicine, and the understanding of the natural world, and these developments fostered a belief in rationalism and empiricism. Against this backdrop, Spiritualism—based on belief in unseen forces and communication with the dead—was seen by many as a throwback to a more superstitious era.

Skeptics often targeted mediums, accusing them of employing trickery to deceive grieving families. There were cases in which fraudulent mediums were exposed, using hidden wires, assistants, or sleight of hand to create the appearance of spirit manifestations. These exposures fueled the narrative that all mediums were charlatans, exploiting the vulnerable for personal gain.

The Fox Sisters themselves, whose Hydesville Rappings had sparked the movement, eventually admitted to fabricating some of the rappings, though the circumstances surrounding their confession remain murky, and some believe they were coerced. Regardless, the controversy surrounding fraud haunted the movement and contributed to its decline in the late 19th century.

Despite this, many mediums and believers continued to defend Spiritualism, arguing that while fraud did exist, it did not invalidate the genuine experiences of countless people who had received comfort and guidance from spirit communication. Prominent figures like Sir Arthur Conan Doyle, the creator of Sherlock Holmes and a devout Spiritualist, became vocal defenders of the movement, engaging in public debates with skeptics.

For me, as a modern medium, the legacy of skepticism is both a challenge and a reminder. I believe that healthy skepticism can coexist with Spiritualism. It's important to question, to seek evidence, and to approach mediumship with both an open mind and a discerning eye. However, I also know that the spirit world operates on a different frequency than the material world, and not everything can be explained or measured by the tools of science.

In my practice, I strive to be as clear and authentic as possible, ensuring that those who come to me for guidance or connection feel secure in the knowledge that I approach my work with integrity. While fraud did exist in the past, it should not overshadow the real and powerful connections that are made between the living and the dead.

Skepticism will always be a part of the conversation surrounding Spiritualism, but it should not be a barrier to exploring the mysteries of the spirit world. Instead, it can be a tool for sharpening our understanding, making sure that we approach our practices with both reverence and care.

The Spread of Spiritualism Across America

After the initial spark ignited by the Fox Sisters in Hydesville, Spiritualism spread like wildfire across America. The movement grew quickly, fueled by a combination of public fascination, personal grief, and the desire for answers to life's biggest questions. In a country still reeling from the devastation of the Civil War and grappling with social and political changes, Spiritualism offered hope and comfort to those who had lost loved ones and sought to understand the mysteries of death and the afterlife.

Séances became common social gatherings in the homes of the wealthy and the working class alike. Spiritualist societies and churches began to form, where mediums would give public demonstrations of their abilities, and the philosophies of the movement were taught and discussed. Spiritualism offered an egalitarian approach to religion, where anyone, regardless of social class or education, could experience divine communication and spiritual growth.

In the post-war period, Spiritualism particularly resonated with those who had lost family members in the Civil War. Widows, mothers, and children who were grieving the deaths of soldiers turned to Spiritualism for comfort, hoping to receive messages from their loved ones in the afterlife. This surge in popularity helped Spiritualism become a prominent religious movement in America during the mid-19th century.

The movement also spread to other parts of the world, particularly to England, where it found a similar audience among those grieving loss and seeking spiritual answers. Internationally, Spiritualism became a transatlantic movement, with mediums and Spiritualist lecturers traveling between Europe and America, spreading the message of life after death.

As a practicing medium, I am constantly aware of the historical roots of Spiritualism in America. The movement's rapid spread is a testament to the universal human desire for connection and understanding beyond the material world. Today, I am part of a long lineage of mediums who continue to offer this connection to those who seek it, helping them find solace and answers in the voices of the spirits.

The Civil War and Spiritualism: Seeking Comfort in a Time of Loss

The American Civil War (1861-1865) was one of the bloodiest and most traumatic conflicts in U.S. history, resulting in the deaths of approximately 620,000 soldiers and untold civilian casualties. Families were torn apart, and the nation was left in deep mourning. During this time, Spiritualism surged in popularity, as grieving families sought solace in the belief that their loved ones were not truly lost but could communicate with them from the afterlife.

For many, the idea that the dead were still present, albeit in spirit form, was a source of profound comfort. Spiritualist mediums offered bereaved families the opportunity to hear from their fallen sons, brothers, and fathers, giving them messages of hope and reassurance. Public séances became more common, and mediums who claimed to contact the spirits of deceased soldiers were in high demand.

In addition to personal loss, the Civil War created a collective national trauma. The sheer scale of death made traditional religious explanations of the afterlife feel insufficient for many. Spiritualism, with its direct communication with the dead, offered a more immediate and personal connection to the afterlife, filling a void left by more conventional religious practices.

Notable figures like Mary Todd Lincoln, the wife of President Abraham Lincoln, were drawn to Spiritualism after the tragic death of their son, Willie, in 1862. Deep in mourning, Mary Lincoln held séances in the White House, seeking to communicate with her lost child. The public fascination

with her engagement in Spiritualism helped to further legitimize the movement in the eyes of many Americans, who
saw her participation as a sign that the practice held genuine power.

For those of us who practice today, the Civil War period
serves as a powerful example of how Spiritualism can provide healing in times of great national and personal grief.
The desire to connect with loved ones who have passed on
is a universal human experience, and during times of
tragedy, the spirit world often feels closer. Even now, I see
how grief can open the heart to spiritual possibilities and
create a bridge between the living and the dead.

Spiritualist Churches: The Institutionaliza-
tion of a Movement

As Spiritualism gained followers across America, it began
to move beyond informal séances and parlor-room gatherings. The next step in the evolution of the movement was
the formation of Spiritualist churches, where believers could
come together in a structured environment to practice their
faith and learn more about the spiritual world.

One of the first Spiritualist organizations was the National Spiritualist Association of Churches (NSAC), founded
in 1893. The NSAC aimed to provide a formal structure for
the growing movement, offering guidelines for mediumship,
promoting the philosophy of Spiritualism, and helping communities establish Spiritualist churches. It also sought to
distinguish Spiritualism from other religious movements,
framing it as a distinct belief system based on the principles
of communication with the dead and the eternal evolution
of the soul.

Spiritualist churches offered weekly services that resem-
bled traditional religious gatherings in some ways but were
distinct in their focus on direct spirit communication. Services often included lectures on Spiritualist philosophy, fol-
lowed by demonstrations of mediumship, where the
church's medium would deliver messages from the spirit
world to the congregation. These messages could be from
deceased loved ones, spiritual guides, or higher entities, and
they were intended to offer comfort, guidance, and insight.

In many ways, the creation of Spiritualist churches
helped to legitimize the movement. By formalizing practices
and establishing a clear set of beliefs, the movement was

able to survive beyond the initial excitement of the Victorian era and continue to thrive into the modern age. Today, Spiritualist churches can be found across the United States and the United Kingdom, continuing to offer a place for those seeking connection with the spirit world.

For me, the existence of Spiritualist churches is a reminder that Spiritualism is not just a practice but a community. The act of gathering together to explore the mysteries of the afterlife and to receive messages from the beyond is a deeply communal experience. Spiritualist churches provide a sacred space for mediums to share their gifts and for believers to receive the healing and comfort that comes from knowing that life continues after death.

Famous Figures of Spiritualism: Mediums and Their Legacies

The Spiritualist movement was propelled forward by many remarkable individuals, both mediums and intellectuals, who shaped its philosophy, practices, and public perception. While some became household names in the Victorian era, their legacies continue to influence Spiritualism today. Among the most influential figures were Andrew Jackson Davis, Cora L. V. Scott, and Emma Hardinge Britten, each of whom brought unique contributions to the movement.

Andrew Jackson Davis, often called the "John the Baptist" of Spiritualism, was a visionary, healer, and clairvoyant who laid much of the philosophical foundation for the movement. Born in 1826, Davis claimed to have had a series of mystical experiences in which he communicated with spirits, including historical figures like Emmanuel Swedenborg and Benjamin Franklin. His book, *The Principles of Nature, Her Divine Revelations, and A Voice to Mankind*, published in 1847, became a cornerstone text for the movement, blending ideas from Mesmerism, Transcendentalism, and Christian mysticism. Davis's work emphasized the interconnectedness of the spiritual and physical realms and the idea that the soul continues to evolve after death.

Cora L. V. Scott was one of the most renowned trance speakers of the 19th century. Known for her eloquent and spontaneous sermons delivered while in a trance state, she became one of the most famous mediums in America. From a young age, Scott traveled the country, speaking on topics ranging from Spiritualist philosophy to women's rights. Her ability to deliver coherent, impassioned speeches while channeling spirits impressed both believers and skeptics alike, cementing her status as a leading figure in the movement.

Emma Hardinge Britten was another key figure in the history of Spiritualism. A medium, writer, and orator, she was one of the earliest chroniclers of the Spiritualist movement. Her book *Modern American Spiritualism*, published in 1870, remains one of the most comprehensive histories of the early years of the movement. Britten was also a staunch advocate for women's rights and social reform, aligning Spiritualism with progressive causes of the time.

For me, these figures represent the diversity and depth of Spiritualism. Each of them contributed something unique to the movement, whether it was through philosophy, public speaking, or advocacy. Their legacies continue to inspire mediums like myself, reminding us that our work is not just about connecting with spirits but about contributing to a larger dialogue about life, death, and the evolution of the soul.

Séances in Popular Culture: The Victorian Obsession

The 19th century was a time of great fascination with the occult, and Spiritualism became deeply woven into the fabric of popular culture. Séances captured the imagination of the public, and they were depicted in literature, theater, and art. This cultural fascination with séances reflected a broader Victorian obsession with death and the afterlife, which was influenced by high mortality rates and a growing interest in the mysteries of the unseen world.

One of the reasons séances became so popular during this period was the combination of scientific advancement and spiritual curiosity. The Industrial Revolution had brought about incredible technological innovations, changing the way people lived and thought about the world. At the same time, these advancements raised new questions about the limits of human knowledge and the mysteries that still lay beyond the reach of science. Spiritualism, with its focus on the unknown and the possibility of contacting the dead, offered a way to explore these mysteries in a tangible and experiential way.

Many Victorian authors, such as Arthur Conan Doyle and Charles Dickens, incorporated elements of Spiritualism into their works. Doyle, a devoted Spiritualist himself, often wrote about mediums and séances, and he used his celebrity status to promote the movement. Dickens, while more skeptical, still explored themes of the supernatural in his works, reflecting the era's deep interest in life beyond death.

Theatrical séances also became a popular form of entertainment. Some mediums turned their séances into public performances, complete with dramatic lighting, mysterious sounds, and levitating objects. These events drew large crowds and were often seen as both religious experiences and theatrical spectacles. While some saw these public séances as genuine spiritual experiences, others viewed them as little more than entertainment.

For me, the cultural depiction of séances in the Victorian era serves as both inspiration and caution. The public fascination with spirit communication during that time is a reminder of how deeply Spiritualism touched the lives of ordinary people. However, it also highlights the tension between genuine mediumship and the potential for exploitation or sensationalism. As a medium, I strive to keep the focus on the healing and wisdom that come from genuine spirit communication, rather than on spectacle.

Mediumship and the Scientific Community: A Contested Field

During the rise of Spiritualism, the scientific community was both fascinated by and skeptical of the claims made by mediums. Many scientists were intrigued by the phenomena reported during séances—such as levitation, voices from beyond, and materializations of spirits—and sought to investigate them using the methods of scientific inquiry. This led to a period where science and Spiritualism intersected, with researchers attempting to validate or debunk mediumistic abilities.

One of the most notable scientific investigations of Spiritualism came from the Society for Psychical Research (SPR), founded in 1882 in London. The SPR aimed to study paranormal phenomena, including Spiritualist practices, using a rigorous scientific approach. Researchers like Sir William Crookes, a respected chemist and physicist, conducted experiments with mediums, hoping to provide empirical evidence of spirit communication. Crookes's experiments with the medium Florence Cook, in particular, garnered significant attention, as he claimed to have witnessed the full materialization of a spirit during a séance.

However, not all scientists were convinced. Many accused mediums of fraud, using tricks and sleight of hand to create the illusion of spirit communication. Harry Houdini, the famous magician and escape artist, was one of the most vocal critics of Spiritualism. After the death of his mother, Houdini sought to contact her through mediums but became disillusioned when he encountered what he believed to be fraudulent practices. He spent much of his later career debunking mediums and exposing the tricks used in séances.

Despite the skepticism, the relationship between Spiritualism and science during the Victorian era was complex. While some scientists sought to discredit the movement, others were genuinely interested in exploring the possibility of life after death. For mediums like myself, this period serves as a reminder that the search for truth often lies at the intersection of belief and inquiry. Today, we continue to explore the mysteries of the spirit world, even as we acknowledge that some aspects of mediumship may remain beyond the reach of conventional science.

The Role of Spiritualism in Social Reform

Throughout its history, Spiritualism has often been associated with social reform movements. In the 19th century, many Spiritualists were also active in causes such as abolitionism, women's suffrage, and temperance. The belief in the moral and spiritual evolution of humanity, a core tenet of Spiritualism, naturally extended to a commitment to social justice and equality.

Spiritualism provided a platform for voices advocating for change. For instance, many prominent Spiritualists were also leading figures in the women's suffrage movement. The idea that women could serve as mediums and spiritual leaders challenged traditional gender roles and demonstrated a broader potential for women's empowerment. Figures like Elizabeth Cady Stanton and Susan B. Anthony, while not Spiritualists themselves, were sympathetic to the movement and recognized its role in promoting women's rights.

The abolitionist movement also found support within Spiritualism. Many Spiritualists were staunchly anti-slavery and saw the movement as part of a broader quest for moral and spiritual enlightenment. The belief in the universal brotherhood of humanity and the idea that spirits from all backgrounds could communicate with the living reinforced the commitment to ending slavery and promoting racial equality.

Similarly, the temperance movement, which sought to reduce or eliminate alcohol consumption, found allies among Spiritualists. The belief in personal and spiritual growth aligned with the goals of temperance reformers, who viewed alcohol as a barrier to moral and spiritual progress. Spiritualist meetings often included discussions on temperance, and many Spiritualist leaders supported the movement's goals.

As a medium, I see the connection between Spiritualism and social reform as a reflection of the movement's broader philosophy. The belief in the continual evolution of the soul and the possibility of spiritual enlightenment naturally extends to a vision of a more just and equitable society. Today, Spiritualist communities continue to engage in social issues, advocating for justice and equality based on the principles of compassion and spiritual growth.

Modern Spiritualism: Adapting to Contemporary Life

Spiritualism, like any religious or philosophical movement, has evolved over time to adapt to the changing world. In the modern era, Spiritualism has undergone significant transformations, incorporating new practices and technologies while retaining its core principles of spirit communication and the eternal nature of the soul.

One of the major changes in modern Spiritualism is the use of technology. The advent of the internet and digital communication has expanded the reach of Spiritualism, allowing mediums to connect with individuals across the globe. Online platforms and virtual séances have become increasingly common, providing a way for people to experience spirit communication even if they are unable to attend in-person events.

Modern Spiritualism also reflects a more diverse range of practices and beliefs. While traditional séances and mediumship remain central to the movement, many Spiritualists now integrate elements from other spiritual and religious traditions. This eclectic approach allows individuals to explore their spirituality in a way that resonates with their personal beliefs and experiences.

Another significant development in modern Spiritualism is the increased focus on personal empowerment and self-development. Many contemporary Spiritualists view the movement not just as a way to communicate with the dead but as a path to personal growth and spiritual enlightenment. Workshops, retreats, and courses on spiritual development are common, helping individuals to enhance their mediumship skills and explore their own spiritual paths.

For me, modern Spiritualism represents both continuity and change. The core beliefs of the movement—such as the existence of an afterlife and the potential for personal growth—remain unchanged, but the ways in which these beliefs are practiced and expressed have evolved. Embracing these changes while staying true to the movement's principles allows Spiritualism to continue to offer comfort, guidance, and insight in a rapidly changing world.

The Science of Mediumship: Exploring the Evidence

The relationship between Spiritualism and science has always been complex, marked by both fascination and skepticism. As mediums continue to practice, the question of whether mediumship can be scientifically validated remains a topic of interest and debate. While many researchers have attempted to study mediumship, the evidence remains largely inconclusive.

One of the challenges in studying mediumship scientifically is the subjective nature of the experience. Mediumship involves personal and spiritual experiences that are difficult to quantify or measure using traditional scientific methods. While some researchers have conducted experiments to test the validity of mediumistic claims, results have often been mixed.

In recent years, there has been a growing interest in exploring the psychological and neurological aspects of mediumship. Researchers have examined how mediums perceive and interpret their experiences, as well as how these experiences might be related to brain function and mental processes. Studies have explored topics such as the role of intuition, the influence of expectation, and the impact of suggestibility on mediumistic communication.

Despite the challenges, some researchers continue to investigate mediumship with an open mind. The goal is not necessarily to prove or disprove the existence of spirits but to understand the nature of mediumistic experiences and their potential significance. For many mediums, including myself, the focus remains on the practical outcomes of mediumship—such as providing comfort and guidance to those seeking connection with the spirit world—rather than on scientific validation.

Ultimately, the question of whether mediumship can be scientifically proven may be less important than the personal and spiritual significance of the experiences themselves. Whether or not science can fully explain mediumship, the value of spirit communication lies in the comfort and insight it provides to those who seek it.

The Global Impact of Spiritualism: A World-wide Movement

While Spiritualism has deep roots in America and England, its impact has extended far beyond these borders. The movement has influenced and been influenced by spiritual and religious traditions across the globe. From Europe to South America to Asia, Spiritualism has found a diverse array of followers and practitioners, each bringing their own cultural perspectives to the movement.

In Europe, Spiritualism gained a foothold in countries such as France, Germany, and Sweden. In France, the mediumship of Allan Kardec, who founded Spiritism, became highly influential. Kardec's writings, including *The Spirits' Book*, offered a systematic approach to understanding the spirit world and contributed to the development of Spiritism as a distinct tradition within Spiritualism.

In South America, Spiritualism has blended with indigenous beliefs and practices to create unique expressions of the movement. Countries like Brazil have a rich tradition of spirit communication, where mediums often work within a framework that combines African, indigenous, and European spiritual elements. Brazilian Spiritualism, known as Umbanda, incorporates elements of Catholicism, African religions, and indigenous traditions, reflecting the diverse cultural landscape of the region.

In Asia, Spiritualism has interacted with traditional spiritual practices and philosophies. In countries like Japan and India, the concept of communicating with spirits has been integrated with local beliefs about the afterlife and spiritual growth. These interactions have enriched the global movement, leading to a variety of practices and interpretations of Spiritualism.

For me, the global reach of Spiritualism is a testament to its universal appeal and relevance. The movement's ability to adapt and integrate with different cultural contexts speaks to its fundamental message—that the connection between the living and the dead is a shared human experience. As a medium, I am continually inspired by the diverse ways in which Spiritualism is practiced around the world, and I strive to honor and incorporate these global perspectives into my own work.

The Challenges Facing Modern Spiritualism

Despite its enduring appeal, modern Spiritualism faces several challenges. As the world changes and new spiritual practices emerge, Spiritualism must navigate a landscape of evolving beliefs and competing interests. Addressing these challenges requires adaptability and a commitment to the core principles of the movement.

One of the main challenges facing Spiritualism is the proliferation of alternative spiritual practices. With the rise of new age spirituality, alternative healing practices, and digital platforms for spiritual exploration, Spiritualism competes for attention and relevance. Many individuals are exploring a wide range of spiritual options, and Spiritualism must find ways to connect with and engage these seekers.

Another challenge is the skepticism and criticism that still surrounds mediumship. Despite advances in understanding and acceptance, many people remain skeptical of spirit communication and question the validity of mediumistic claims. This skepticism can lead to misunderstandings and misrepresentations of the movement, making it important for Spiritualists to communicate clearly and honestly about their practices and beliefs.

Additionally, the commercialization of Spiritualism can be a concern. As the movement gains visibility, there is a risk of exploitation and sensationalism. It is essential for Spiritualists to maintain the integrity of their practices and ensure that the focus remains on genuine spirit communication and healing rather than on profit or spectacle.

For me, these challenges are opportunities to reaffirm the core values of Spiritualism. By staying true to the principles of compassion, integrity, and spiritual growth, Spiritualists can continue to offer meaningful experiences and insights. Addressing these challenges with openness and creativity allows the movement to evolve and thrive in a changing world.

The Future of Spiritualism: Looking Ahead

As we look to the future, the evolution of Spiritualism will be shaped by ongoing changes in society, technology, and spiritual exploration. The movement's ability to adapt and remain relevant will depend on its capacity to embrace new developments while staying true to its foundational principles.

One potential area of growth for Spiritualism is the integration of new technologies. Virtual reality, artificial intelligence, and other technological innovations offer exciting possibilities for enhancing the practice of mediumship and reaching new audiences. These technologies could provide new ways to experience spirit communication and explore the mysteries of the afterlife.

Another important aspect of Spiritualism's future is its continued engagement with diverse cultural perspectives. As the movement becomes more global, it will benefit from incorporating and respecting the spiritual traditions of different cultures. This cross-cultural exchange can enrich the practice of Spiritualism and foster greater understanding and unity among spiritual seekers.

The future of Spiritualism will also involve a renewed focus on personal and collective spiritual growth. As individuals seek deeper meaning and connection in their lives, Spiritualism can offer guidance and support for personal transformation and self-discovery. By emphasizing the importance of spiritual development and inner growth, the movement can continue to inspire and uplift those who seek it.

For me, the future of Spiritualism is filled with promise and potential. By embracing change while honoring the movement's core values, Spiritualism can continue to offer profound insights and comfort to those who seek to connect with the spirit world. As we move forward, I am excited to be part of a community that is committed to exploring the mysteries of existence and supporting the spiritual journey of every individual.

Personal Reflections: My Journey as a Medium

As a practicing medium, my journey has been deeply intertwined with the history and evolution of Spiritualism. Each séance, each communication with the spirit world, is a continuation of the path that began with the Fox Sisters and the birth of the movement. My experiences as a medium have shaped my understanding of Spiritualism and deepened my connection to the spirit world.

One of the most profound aspects of my work is the ability to offer comfort and guidance to those who are grieving. The messages I receive from the spirits often provide solace and hope to individuals who have lost loved ones. Witnessing the impact of these messages is a reminder of the importance and value of mediumship in helping people navigate their grief and find peace.

Another significant part of my journey has been the ongoing exploration of my own spiritual growth. Each interaction with the spirit world provides new insights and lessons, contributing to my personal development and understanding of the afterlife. This process of learning and evolving is central to my practice as a medium and is a reflection of the broader philosophy of Spiritualism.

As I look back on my experiences, I am grateful for the opportunity to be part of a tradition that offers so much to those who seek it. The connections I have made with the spirit world and the people I have encountered through my work are a testament to the enduring relevance and significance of Spiritualism. My journey as a medium continues to

be a source of inspiration and fulfillment, and I am honored
to share it with others.

Spiritualism and Art: Creative Expressions of the Movement

Art has always played a significant role in expressing and exploring spiritual themes. Spiritualism, with its focus on the connection between the living and the dead, has inspired a range of artistic expressions that capture the movement's essence and impact. From literature to visual arts to performance, Spiritualism has influenced and been influenced by creative endeavors.

In literature, Spiritualism has been a recurring theme, with authors exploring the mysteries of the spirit world and the afterlife. Writers such as Arthur Conan Doyle, who was a prominent Spiritualist, incorporated spiritual themes into their works. Doyle's "The Spiritualist" and other writings reflect his fascination with mediumship and his belief in the reality of the spirit world.

Visual arts have also been a medium for expressing Spiritualist ideas. Artists such as George Inness and James Whistler have created works that reflect their interest in spiritual and metaphysical themes. Their paintings often evoke a sense of the transcendent and the connection between the material and spiritual realms.

Performance art, including theater and film, has explored Spiritualism's dramatic and emotional aspects. Productions that feature mediums, séances, and spirit communication offer audiences a glimpse into the world of Spiritualism and its impact on the imagination. These creative expressions contribute to the broader cultural understanding of Spiritualism and its significance.

For me, art is a powerful way to convey the experiences and insights gained through mediumship. The creative process allows for a deeper exploration of spiritual themes and provides a means of sharing the beauty and mystery of the spirit world with others. By engaging with art, Spiritualism can continue to inspire and captivate the imagination of people across different cultures and generations.

Spiritualism in Popular Culture: Media and Representation

The portrayal of Spiritualism in popular culture has evolved over time, reflecting changing attitudes and interests. From early stage performances to contemporary films and television shows, Spiritualism has been a subject of fascination and intrigue in the media. These representations have both shaped and been shaped by public perceptions of the movement.

In the early 20th century, Spiritualism was often depicted in melodramatic and sensationalized terms. Stage performances and early films frequently portrayed séances and mediumship with an emphasis on the mysterious and supernatural. These depictions contributed to the public's fascination with the spirit world but also reinforced stereotypes and misconceptions about the movement.

As media representations of Spiritualism have evolved, there has been a growing interest in exploring its more nuanced aspects. Contemporary films, television shows, and books often present Spiritualism in a more complex and balanced light. These modern portrayals may address themes of grief, healing, and personal growth, offering a more nuanced understanding of the movement.

Popular culture also reflects the diverse ways in which Spiritualism is practiced and experienced. Media representations can highlight the variety of practices within Spiritualism, from traditional séances to modern spiritual workshops. This diversity allows for a broader exploration of the movement and its impact on individuals and communities.

For me, the representation of Spiritualism in popular culture is both a reflection of and an influence on the movement's public image. By engaging with media portrayals, we can gain insight into how Spiritualism is perceived and understood by different audiences. It also offers an opportunity to share the true essence of the movement and its significance in a way that resonates with contemporary audiences.

Conclusion: The Legacy of Victorian Spiritualism

Victorian Spiritualism, with its rich history and profound impact, continues to be a source of inspiration and exploration. From its origins with the Fox Sisters to its modern expressions, the movement has evolved and adapted while staying true to its core principles of spirit communication and the eternal nature of the soul.

As a medium, I am deeply connected to this legacy. The experiences and insights gained through mediumship reflect the enduring relevance of Spiritualism and its ability to offer comfort, guidance, and spiritual growth. The principles of Spiritualism—such as the belief in an afterlife, the potential for personal evolution, and the importance of compassion—continue to resonate with those who seek connection with the spirit world.

Looking ahead, the future of Spiritualism holds both challenges and opportunities. As the movement navigates a changing world, it will need to embrace new technologies, engage with diverse cultural perspectives, and address evolving societal needs. By staying true to its core values and adapting to new developments, Spiritualism can continue to offer meaningful experiences and insights to those who seek it.

The legacy of Victorian Spiritualism is a testament to the enduring quest for understanding and connection between the living and the dead. It is a journey that continues to inspire and uplift, offering hope and wisdom from the spirit world. As we move forward, we carry with us the lessons and insights of the past, honoring the rich history of Spiritualism while embracing the possibilities of the future.